Tiny, Frantic, Stronger

Tiny, Frantic, Stronger
Jeff Latosik

INSOMNIAC PRESS

Library and Archives Canada Cataloguing in Publication

Latosik, Jeff
Tiny, frantic, stronger / Jeff Latosik.

Poems.
ISBN 978-1-897178-95-9

I. Title.
PS8623.A788T56 2010   C811'.6   C2010-900691-7

The publisher gratefully acknowledges the support of the Canada Council, the
Ontario Arts Council, and the
Department of Canadian Heritage through the Book
Publishing Industry Development Program.

Printed and bound in Canada

Insomniac Press
520 Princess Ave.,
London, Ontario, Canada, N6B 2B8
www.insomniacpress.com

Canada Council   Conseil des Arts
for the Arts   du Canada

ONTARIO ARTS COUNCIL
CONSEIL DES ARTS DE L'ONTARI

Canadä

for William Burch

Contents

Rollant hath set the olifant to his mouth,
He grasps it well, and with great virtue sounds.
High are those peaks, afar it rings and loud,
Thirty great leagues they hear its echoes mount.

—*Song of Roland*

1.

How the Tiktaalik Came onto Land

Something caught. A stronger jaw,
a first digit, a current sweeping the smaller
thriving prey to shallow water.

Devonian fluke. Nothing simply walked out;
nothing wriggled quite like doubt
on a bare corkboard of thought,

so we pinned it down, with gusto.
A theory goes that vascular leaves
were shedding in the subtropics,

twining and spreading like fishing nets.
A theory goes something more than blood and scales
was needed to stay anchored in the undertow.

A theory floats, raises sail.
It moves on water that twists
and breaks against itself like a losing team.

A dynasty sets. I wanted to say I regret
not having played more baseball.
I wanted to say you've been gone a long time

for going to get milk, five minutes you said,
and here are your keys
and the doors they open like traps.

Toronto Island, Summer

We were scared to swim because of what was down there.
We were down there.

Or, we counted everything that could be dumped
from our vast reservoirs of taste: magazines, subway ads,
Hollywood movies that bobbed like buoys in our conversation.

We listed our favourite natural disasters.
We heard some kids had swum out past the roped-in shallows,
so we booked it over, expectations dog-paddling their way
through reasons against, even hate.

But there was nothing to hate. Only a cold wind, rain,
some past indiscretions that stung
like fastballs from a fastball machine. Coming through a clearing,
we saw their clothes piled in the sand, now, just evidence.
Water the colour of a botched photograph.

They were out there
in the undeveloped punching
whitecaps, pushing on. The city behind them,
spread out like a row of chess pieces,
like we could rearrange it with our breath.

Eight Kinds of Knots

A streetcar stalled on Howard Park
and Roncesvalles Ave. Passengers cleared,

they fume in sunlight, waiting for a newer version
of the part that held their afternoon together.

It's heading towards them at half the speed
of a newly launched home run in the park,

and the crowd can make a dome of their cheering.
Close by, a first-grade field trip watches,

teachers blossoming consent forms. Lined up
crooked, two by two, these kids are a living long division.

Arguing over who will be an astronaut first, one flips a coin,
another waits, while the traffic starts backing up,

the banks get full and a man walks around with a hammer
unsure of what to do with it. In his pocket he motions

another figure eight: that's a hard one to pull apart,
but he does. The rolling hitch—slip the frayed end under the slack,

tighten, slack, tighten, slack,
until the Scotch tape on our LOST CAT signs peels

back, until a glass bottle falls from a ledge, it gets dark,
and every lit up window is a difficult board game.

Later, a raccoon scattering newspaper
over the road, the headlights that scare him under a deck,

the fold-out chairs that won't fold back.
If you listen you can hear someone talking about the last time

she climbed a fence and in how many places her wrist broke.
And the planes seem closer, the stars, countable.

An Unauthorized Account of the Downtime of the Lovely Couple

Night pushed their windows closer.
They slouched more. It felt good to give up posture.

They sat for hours, immersed in a game
that involved a series of miniature doors.

The problem was figuring out who was winning
or when the game might come to an end.

I imagined my life differently, she said.

No matter, he said, when I drink
I'm the tallest man in Toronto.

There was the ritual of high-fiving
until something delicate fell from a table.

There was inhaling the price tags from beautiful clothes.

You have too many tiny apartments, she said.

And he sat on the chair he'd made for her
from balsa wood, remembered how it all came
in dusty panels with uneven edges,
how he'd told her that was the measure of awe,
cutting panels from larger panels

as if somewhere at the start of it
there was something huge and complete.

Collapsible Range

This newer model runs on half
the maybe-we-should-next-year guilt.
    This newer model's easily folded
for storage or travel, clouds permitting.
Not permitting this model's reliance
on user assistance has been ironed out.

    To lift the latch. To let contentment
hitch up its trailer and ride around—
No errors reported. No pending lawsuits.
    Developed from research that piled high,
so we slid the thought of it aside like a chair.
    Once, I dropped one down the stairs
    and it played soft rock for half an hour.

Available in six soothing colours excluding red,
known to incite some mice to gnawing
as if our mazes were trying to escape them.
    Newer models have been conceived
completely free of extraneous weight.
    They grind along throughout the day
    and are only noticed when turned off.
    But how they recede. How dim and half-done.

Police

The easy option is always blaring
from a megaphone. A genius of shortcuts,
it can't be shaken. At night I hear a suitcase
clicking shut, opening. But outside
there is just the city: its patrons, parks,
limousines without any doors. Morning
will resuscitate the buildings. You're on the bed,
trying to go the longest without talking.
I say you do not need to talk,
but that does not make me the winner.
In the parking lot, a police car, idling,
its laptop glowing in the dark.

Walk-in

Discuss the severity of your symptoms.
On a scale of one to twenty-five,
plot your level of discomfort
as if the worst were a gunshot wound.

On a scale of one to twenty-five,
the probability of having been shot
is worse off than a gunshot wound,
but try to imagine it anyways—

and it's probable that, having been shot,
you'd sense there isn't much feeling
right away, you imagine numbness
flooding where the pain's too much

or where it can't be fully sensed.
But, still, imagine, for our purposes—
to flood out the source of the pain—
that such a continuum is plain,

and also imagine, if you can,
the bottom end as a minor pinch.
The continuum's plane is gradually sloped
to accommodate this.

Don't worry: this will end in a pinch.
If you're still confused, or if it seems
unaccommodating to talk like this,
think only of how you want to get better—

still confused, the picture seems
to fill in more with each new piece of information.
Think only of how you want to get better.
Let that be your daily mantra.

Though each new piece of information
requires discussion of your symptoms,
remember that even a daily mantra
may cause a level of discomfort.

Helping

Cars drive in and drive out,
gone. Sandra's back
with gin on her dress.

What's stretched
between us continues stretching,
a zoom lens.

Look inside and watch
whole neighbourhoods
sink into grids.

I want to help her,
but she won't stay—
no one can keep up with her.

The wind from the south
is warmer now. The not-quite
pushes against us too.

Sunnyside

Here, condos go up and up,
and even trees seem to nod.
Legs feel like liabilities in new jeans;
she's trying to forget that.
Beneath, a boy acts out
an unbearable series of buzzer-beaters.
She loses count. Stands, stretches.
The skyline lengthens in her necklace.

Problem is when you haven't decided,
all the options are partly yours.
She could stay with him;
she could walk towards the newly funded
city bridge, its splash of cables.
There, a quiet murmuring sound,
like someone speaking under water.
Here, a slide, a hinge, a fence.

Maybe some of the world has settled
and can't be shaken loose.
The way she imagines a coastal shelf
trying to reach beyond itself—
or how the villains in old B movies
seemed poised to conquer their cut-out cities,
but then some glaring weakness
poured up like a wellspring through them.

The Backwards Builders

The backwards builders take apart
your house. They start at your porch,
unzip the wood, leave the deck chairs
shrugging their shoulders—

then they move closer, level the doors
that let the private hunker down
and hang its prints. The knob
in the next room, a hallway flutters,

you want to tell them stop,
but a door closes in your mouth.
They continue breaking hinge
from hinge, beam from beam,

the visible from what can't be seen
by simply looking. Now they've pulled
out the basement that was in the brick
and now they're breaking windows

in a nucleus. The pieces drop away
and divorce each other many times;
then the backwards builders yank
the drawstrings on electrons

so they go spinning up like blinds.
Something emerges: Clouds.
A scribble. The edge of a wing.
Tear gas. Tear gas. Turn signal.

2.

Freddy Krueger Blues
for db

I wish my childhood fears were true:
that scalded men with knives for fingers
waited in the darkest corners of the room.

Cackling men whose intentions bent like Plasticine
around the curvature of my worry: kidnappings, homework, too-
    tight pants—
men who shoved absence closer with every step.

I'd owe a debt of thanks to them, for taking an interest
in my suffering, for making a funhouse of malevolence
where every cruel attack came custom-made.

Now I lie awake at night, composing letters to people
I haven't spoke to in years, wanting to snap
the tent of longing open for a few hours.

Who would have known the thing to watch out for
wasn't knived fingers, scalded men with strange vendettas,
but getting too comfortable,

plugging your ears and whispering no,
no, there is a man here who will not let me leave the room,
can't you see him moving by the shadows on the wall?

Tiny Theatres

We loved how theatres kept getting smaller, how they dwindled down with ostentation. My wristwatch could even be a theatre! Yes, we lapped up what was coming. With all the speed of a scorched asteroid, we took our love interests down into the spacious darkness of our basements. That was the new Friday night haunt, a place where we could loose the rusting plot holes of our lives like bottle caps. *Pop! Ping!* The ping of a perfect one-liner; the sort of yellow afterglow like a line of applauding street lights. We loved sitting in the sticky aisles of an old storyline, how the paint cans, hammers and unshelved trophies got shoved aside by the opening credits, and the image kept taking off its clothes so we could see what was being said right there, like gravy being poured on porcelain. If you took a tiny theatre apart you could see it was a town of highways and malls, the batteries all angled like churches. You could see our heroes cruising the one-way streets of victory. I liked how the smallness took more of the glare away. I wanted whatever was lukewarm and waiting. And when I came for vengeance, I wanted vengeance, so why did it all just twist like a blockbuster ending, a smushed sheet of tinfoil, in the soft and anonymous breeze?

Sonnet for Fake Puke

Pea soup, oatmeal, flour, yeast—
mixed and shaken can put the repulsive
on display, create a distance
that keeps us seated. To play hooky,
to give the scene an air of danger,
the joke store's version is second rate…

At Discount Aquarium Store, a shark
swims the length of its thousand-gallon tank
over and over, through the shit
and half-chewed food that won't bleach.
Three feet long and living on the fish
tossed in every night at five p.m., it moves
like the dot in karaoke and we gather around it,
press our fists against the glass.

The Rise and Fall of the Station Wagon

Fake wood panelling, fake wood dash,
fake wood in the crosses that hung from mirrors.
The real wood creaked, rotted, cracked.

Real wood was like pouring buckets of tar
over the pristine game-show winnings.
Every year the trunk got bigger, full of their trophies,

their tools, dying trees that needed to be wrapped in blankets.
Like the frame was made of Plasticine. Like Plasticine
was made of the thing they were pressing the pedal to the metal for.

Their kids took it out for a spin, past fences, lines.
When they turned too hard, or hit some ice,
or when the driver saw for one brief flash

something across the median that looked like money,
the back spun out like the hand of a clock
in a sped-up movie sequence. They were driven back

in separate ambulances, each vehicle with its party hat.
And there was a song on the radio, the driver's favourite,
and then he thought that maybe this was a different song.

"Incongruous places often inspire anomalous stories."
—*Stephen Jay Gould*

1.

Quiet audience of minutes. Packets of sugar,
the fridge makes ice.

We're very small. Afternoons I spent
in demo home theatres, pretending I'd buy.

Men in camouflage firing and firing
their way to the pop song that came with the credits.

I went home and packed. Slid my hand
in an old Nintendo. Sometimes my actions are not digestible.

2.

Recognition's gauze thins, tears. Wrap it tighter.
Wipe out and a version slips from you like a shirt.

Nobody on Queen Street listens to my bell.
Parking meters, children, men who don't budge—

to bike through, sunburnt, swerving to avoid
a dog freed from the mercy of its leash.

I wanted it grease-proof. I wanted a label
with a white sand beach. Every parked car is a door that might.

3.

We've travelled too far. Little accidents make their empires.
A panel considers the panel's trustworthiness.

Why's it so hard to make arrangements with your shelves?
On bigger screens the protagonist lucks out.

He prioritizes well. He carries a flashlight in his back pocket.
He says things like: I love the anchorman's hair in the wind.

Or: If you can't tell who the sucker is, it's you.
Or: I never said you had to. I only said think of the profit.

No One Spoke of Caleb

No one spoke of Caleb
in polished kitchens, living rooms of applause and plush,
the balcony every father heaved a silver barbeque onto.

Sirens rolled us from our sleep.
Mothers filled glass bowls with Aspirin,
and though they told us not to play catch with snow globes,
we played catch, until they turned the colour of soot.

In school we learned about circulation,
veins that stretched like highways in us,
carrying goods: blood cells, oxygen, which carried carbon,
and the heart, cut loose,
resembled something wrapped in leaves.

January was a slapshot, purple mouth on our shins.
Caleb didn't let a single goal through his pads.
Night came; our TV dinners fell.

Something Inside That Grows Like a Vine

Something inside that grows like a vine
over the brickwork of understanding.
There will be times of confusion.

An urge to start again. To change your name,
when the subway comes like a long, moody
thing inside that grows like a vine.

A misplaced wallet. Rifling through your wrinkled
clothes, taking a bus as far as it'll go, there will be lust,
and there will be times of confusion.

The cold that comes when winter's thumb
is pressing down. Liking it and liking
something inside that grows like a vine.

The TV at the café is an aquarium
of updates. We have to try to keep our best selves alive.
There will be times of confusion.

A crowd of someone else's details
gathering around you, becoming your details,
growing inside you like a vine,
growing like times of confusion.

Song for the Field Behind Mississauga Valley Public School

The field that stretched beyond
goalposts. The field that redrew
lines in us.

Like the field in a glove save.
A high-five. The field in a radio hit,
its raised seating.

Or, the field in waiting. The field in hunger.
The field in a fifth beer, a wrong turn,
the field in the little scar
on your neighbour's forehead.

The field in every abandoned thing
we found in that field. In every bent putter.
Torn jacket. Set of keys.
The field in forgetting. In debt.

Windows

The ripple and splash of rain on the blurred glass
Seemed that it briefly said, as I walked by,
Something I should have liked to say to you
—Howard Nemerov

They're unloading windows from a company truck.
Double-panel. A pile grows like a glass hedge
    by the doorway of the furniture store.

I'm in the café, ordering another, drawing
a maze on a newspaper article. In the centre
    of it something about grief

or the human genome. Look how the windows
persuade us we're right. One neat stack, tall as a child.
    They keep piling windows

like a film stuck on fast-forward, where no one
ever looks unsure. A waitress pulls a crumpled flower
    from her pouch,

gives a petal to a man who shoves it deep inside his pocket.
So many windows. Some hinges are old and shouldn't be tested
    by sudden jerks or cold weather.

A crowd is gathering outside, rubbing their hands.
It's become a spectacle, this slow regimen.
    The structure wobbles, shakes,

steadies. Now it stands taller than us. People whisper
to one another. Some laugh. Some are wearing sunglasses
    and pointing to the sky.

Windsurfing Fathers

Their sons are pointed anchors
that flip over onto delicate canvas.

Tearing through residential streets
in bright vans, the windsurfing fathers
curse left turns and child support.

Sons as dull as a garage door
or a white fence: quiet, cautious, never
disobedient—

they wait in parking lots
while their fathers
stand on oceans, like myths.

Doubt

That comes on like a flurry of bills
that you can't pay. So you take up yoga

or drawing palm trees on the backs of napkins.
That doesn't regress. Brakes failing,

or a room in which something terrible is said.
Partly comfort. Admit it, your crux.

As if worry could sling your mind's arm,
make a fortress of what could and isn't.

So later as you watch a child
on a swing set, shouting "higher," you think *jerk*—

like his feet could shatter the sky like a glass cupboard.
He tells you "coward." Because there is no other word.

Because desire swerves one way, the world another.
Because the bolts hold. The joists loosen. You get better.

3.

The Disappearance Suite

This one would be the masterpiece.
They rented a cabin somewhere in a chain
of mountains that looked like Braille
when viewed from the plane.

Formerly known as Marry My Grace,
they were now The Corridors.
A critic had recently described their music
as a stalled gondola overlooking a snack bar.

Three members: Leiv, Shraun and Kal.
Leiv was learning every guitar solo from 1970 to 1972.
Shraun said that an album's sixth song
was an unmined chance to change coordinates.

And Kal had started, somehow, to fade,
like the closing bars of an '80s hit.
A rare condition "fadeawayitis,"
it had only been observed in obscure German films.

Days leaned against the crowd fence of other days.
Each new chorus seemed to suggest another,
like going back on a genealogy tree,
until it seemed each song comprised its own album.

Friends suggested kidnapping plots
and erratic behaviour on Kal's absence.
A helicopter flew through a forest,
and local news stations ran exposés

concluding the madman was still at large.
Some candlelit vigils were reported
with a hometown focus, but it was uncertain
whether the footage was borrowed or shot.

But in tune with some rarer frequency,
The Corridors knew the truth: that Kal had turned
the knob too high on his own track
and had slipped into a feed that would not come back.

Plea to a Dentist for More Freezing

1.

Five men build a brick wall
in the middle of the road.
They stop, unload, wave cars by.

The wall gets high.

Nobody thinks of how to get down.

What's important is the wall,
a monument now. Standing there,
our cavities getting slightly deeper
like questions at a press conference,
we approve the wall. We can't imagine
what it was like before.

2.

Don't think that I'm ungrateful
for the needle, the Tylenol 3–grade small talk,
the fluff piece of your ceiling fan—

just tell me, in terms of percentages,
how many more percentages do I need?

No, that is not what I mean. Look outside:
people are walking briskly to the industrious
province of coffee. Beauty is an endless kneeling and drinking
from television cables. The weather's fine,
or the pleasure's yours,

or I'm a new, more tired person.

3.

Tell me about my tooth-whitening options.

Tell me there's a veneer for every skewed angle.

One of your speakers is leaking syrup.

Don't ask me how I got in this mess.

There is more news: yesterday, an ice cream truck
crashed into an ice cream store and the first thing
it did was lower prices. There are twenty-seven bones
in the human hand and twenty-seven billboards in a morning.

4.

Ten people train in fireman school.

In the parking lot across the street
they navigate pylons,
squeeze through tires,
carry dolls in human likeness
while someone yells inaudible commands into a megaphone.

If they have to fight fires at an obstacle course,
they'll be ready.

Not knowing what's coming next
is like being the only one who shows up with wine.

5.

Dr. Baxter, wipe my thoughts from me,
like handprints from a window.

Though deemed safe, reports suggest
the joists' constant flex is caused by unforeseen
and complicated variables.

There are many adjustments to make.
The radio is on and tallies are going up
like condos by a nice body of water.

Maybe there were things we could have done better.

What do I mean? Oh, Dr. Baxter, you said the pinching
would only be slight. You said the bill would be covered.
You said that there would be a brochure
for what to do after. And then another helicopter landed.

Song for Tinnitus

I saw a television advertisement recently for a new product called an air sanitizer. A woman stood in her kitchen, spraying the empty space in front of her as though using Mace against an imaginary assailant. She appeared very determined.
—The New York Times

You were there
but you weren't there
a bad signal
you never left
I may have damaged
too much
but still you couldn't be
reasoned with
you came back
when I listened less
you got louder
it was hard
to say exactly
how you sounded
not a siren
not a hiss
it was hard to say
the colour of the river
a cloud approached
our guesses bruised
it was hard to say
what was ahead
an assailant
or scrap, a few
dead branches.

Song for Suspect Video

Spring. The trees are all through
to the next round. Nostalgia unpacks
its patio set and we sit, gladly.
There's a kind of wind
that rounds corners like bad news.
Part of Queen West burns down
while people sleep, and all afternoon
the lecture of drilling.

Sometimes she can almost see
like embers crackling near a flame,
a now-gone store, a now-gone sign.
Sometimes she can almost see
in an empty loft
two people unpacking
or getting dressed. Two people
circling each other, like goldfish.

The Sidewalk Quicksand
for Spike

You got pulled—or was it me?—
into the sidewalk quicksand.
Spat out an hour earlier and still

revved up to dent the lead of our boredom.
But having emerged, one of us
was too far behind:

that hour mushroom-clouded its way
into years, like a navigator
missing the mark by one tenth.

If you got stuck there now,
I would give you anything,
my hands, my hair, to keep you here,

and possibly you would be kept,
the day going museum dim,
your hands getting crushed, and crushing.

Cottages

He feels it moving through his arm: lightning!
Jerks his hand from the gushing tap
and runs to where his mother is knitting
toques in the sunroom. She's watching
the storm pass over them, eating marshmallows
from a bowl she made before he was born.

High above them, the rumbling birth
of clouds like fists. And the lightning's
arm, as if searching for the marshmallows
the boy clutches, his fingers tapping.
The mother doesn't stop, keeps watching
the heavy rain. Her vacation knitting

calmer than her back-home knitting,
which is a kind of suffering born
from keeping the TV on without watching—
here she finds the view enlightening,
is not averse to watching him practice tap-
dancing with a bag of marshmallows

on his head. Those same marshmallows
messing the couch. She goes on knitting.
She could open her admonitions like a tap
and chide the boy, *you know you weren't born
yesterday*, and as she thinks this, lightning
strikes, this time closer, and she watches.

She notices too the boy is watching,
his face expressionless as a marshmallow.
He tells her that he felt that lightning
in his arm, and why doesn't she stop her knitting
and listen closely? The radio says: *the birth
of a hurricane*. When their attention is tapped,

the mother goes and turns off the tap.
Still expressionless, the boy watches,
and though the rain lets up, there's nothing born
from this demonstration, only the marshmallows
trembling on the table, and half-finished knitting.
After, one last flash of lightning.

She shelves her knitting, finds a marshmallow.
The tap glints, and the boy watches
the birth of some new, closer lightning.

The Piñata

They came to strike the piñata.
The piñata hung from a crane
and swayed, its swollen gut
of newspaper and paste.
They listened as the piñata creaked,
a dock in choppy waters.
They began to shout themselves to the brink.
And standing there, watching the piñata,
it seemed almost possible
to forget the search that had continued
since Christmas, was it this one
or the one before?
Parks, rivers, cupboards, drawers,
the bent light beneath their decks—
what had they found?
And standing there, the piñata swaying,
they were gathered and ready
with hammers, bats, knives and chains
to smash and tear until the piñata's shanks
could be nipped by dogs.
Though when the first seam split,
some resorted to doubling over
and pawing the grass.
While others continued taking swings,
the halved ones moved with new insistence,
their hands sweeping over the ground
like visible winds.

Misfortune Drove a 1956 Buick Convertible
for George Latosik

As if all the underlines you ever made
shook free of their books,
and formed a line that highlighted nothing,

or as if your dead seahorses drifted
like balloons back to the tanks
you kept like a last great hope of shores.

As if your knee shattered
so many times it became whole again,
and what poison your body made

was squeezed from the ten-ply sponge
of your thigh. As if a tree could not shade its killer,
or grow through a fence,

or all the doors you abandoned in scrapyards
wobbled into their original hinges.
As if misfortune drove a 1956 Buick convertible

into a wall of its own misfortune,
or all the Queen West condos were gutted
and turned back into factories

and men were praised for fighting in alleys,
and you never learned to tell time by the soreness in your hands.
As if a plume of smoke receded into its fire,

like a crowd of people boarding a train,
and children were sleeping, and the city was quiet,
and the only man there to see it was too busy burning papers.

Cockroach Elegy

Who came like a rumour of gold.

Who burrowed through shelving, drywall, plaster,
and hung their hats on what had rotted. Who made
a palace of the cracks in things.

Whose sun was the absence of sun.

Whose bank was crumbs and balances.

Who got stomped on, smashed, stubbed out, sheared,
poisoned, halved, whose bodies twitched
on kitchen tiles like speedometers.

Whose mind was an old-time music box,
whose hunger was fifty children playing soccer
on an unmarked field.

Who gave birth like a machine gun firing,
whose lineage took the long train from the Cretaceous,
who continue scurrying away from us, tiny, frantic, stronger.

Silverfish Elegy

Silverfish hold the house together.
Pull them out, and the frame falls around itself
like an empty shirt.

They aren't distributed evenly.
Some are falling around themselves,
their own clasps having given;
some move further into the nourishing dark.

All the pressure points are moving
through the house, congealing, cracking.

At the table someone sits and thinks
of how to deliver the news.
It is not good; a door will slam;
a wristwatch will go missing.

Under him, a different pace,
life that is measured in days
or seconds, and floorboards that last.

Centipede Elegy

Caught inside a tissue fist,
they writhe and struggle
without abandon; they are never through.
Even with thirty broken legs,

they see no reason to fold it in.
Their lives are given no second thought:

they're trying one moment;
then they're not.

Nothing of note is recorded.

Yet they'll go on precisely
because they don't matter.

Their too-long legs; their ridged backs
as if knocked flat by some blunt tool—

crush them hard so they don't
wiggle into the hole in your finger.

Or leave them for some other track.
The timer is on. The stove, lit.
You'll have to find another way.

4.

Dolphin

for Tim

When the gauge broke, something
else broke: there was only static,
flitting out.

Earlier, a satellite map displayed
wind speed in primary colours.
The storm's name would alternate back.

And when it crashed through,
the hotel bent, as if a mould
hadn't set properly.

Some flexed their biceps
surreptitiously. Some combed
their hair with their hands.

When it was done, they found a dolphin
washed up on the balcony of room 200—
what to do but make a bed

of complimentary towels?
When they lifted, the dolphin creaked,
like a hard-to-reach beam bearing weight.

Then they were up to their waists
and looking back, the burnt-out signs.
And when the water got too fast

and strong to do anything but kick,
they couldn't hold their good intent
to push it the rest of the way.

Bridges

for Abysmal Daze

Without them, the song backflips off the guardrail of its being there.
A perfect chorus and the loneliness after.

Being fifteen, rail-thin, we had only
our band and the taut tuned string of an afternoon.
The heft and drag of what we hauled: cymbals, amps, third-tier
Strats with awful action. Tossed pillows in the bruised cheek of a
    bass drum,
quelling the complaint of every loose surface. A round of tuning,
letting our fingers unpack their knapsack of mistakes.
Then Fraser, pounding rhythm in the mess of feedback, clipped ex
    changes,
a bass line, stumbling, as if about to bum a smoke.

To get that going, makeshift engine of C G F, filling it out
from needy verse to solipsistic solo. To bring it to
where creation feigns collapse and finger-tapping is an option.
Outside, the hot drone, with its highways of debt, whatever could
    be added
to a patio being added.
Textbooks propped against the door that shut us in: heavy unread
stacks of equations, their longer derivative set.

I'll Climb the Tree If You Climb the Tree

Tomorrow will come, dressed in newspaper
balancing a phone book. Tomorrow will come
like a valid point opposing a valid argument.

I walk around the house, turning off lights.
Boys assume they'll outlive their fathers
as lakes freeze, snow appraises the house and turns back.

Look in my eyes: you can see my talent for flagging taxis—
that I'll give a dollar even if the charge was fifty cents.
Tomorrow will wither, will tear a sleeve of thought,

will try to make a pact with your worst mistake.
And if we were younger, we'd wriggle out.
But we lack knapsacks and a knowledge of getaway paths.

So I'll climb the tree if you climb the tree.
The branches are cold, clothed in snow. But we must climb.
Higher is a harness when all you see are branches.

Let's Go to the Park

I wanted to.
I just couldn't find an escalator.
Don't be the guy from the soap commercial
who can't be wrong. There was a calendar
in my arms made of oak, heavy.

Forget the date, the smell of primer, paint, glue.
Bring a hat. Billboards are thirty-five degrees and rising.

Fresco or mural, cheese or double cheese
leaving now or boycotting later—

Let's go to the park.
We can make a bird from a silver wrapper.
The facts blow south. I meant wind.

Look, the baseball team is warming up,
they climb and climb the dugout fence.
Number thirty runs for a fly, keeps on running,
all the way out of sight.

A little rain, a sudden gust.
That plastic watch we found ticking
away to its imperfect end.
Someone we knew walks into our thoughts
while a car drives off, a dog barks,
a woman feeds the smashed pigeons.

Cactus Love

The cactus keeping its cool water secret
is simple to love: as if all that is hard in us,
closed up as tight as a fist in a pocket
can still be loved, need not be relieved.

To prick your thumb, to call that conversation,
in a quiet room when you're tired of speaking
and someone you've kissed all light from
is curled under a blanket in her own wrinkled mood.

The cactus, which thrives in irascible sunlight,
cracked earth and stone. Calm as a soldier's
silent sleeves. The cactus knows there is
even a war in the cracks between stones.

The cactus leaning into February sun:
a long green tongue that never tells us
yes or no. To have brushed the webs from
its tiny perfect spikes and considered forgiveness.

One blue flower that closes like a door
when Spring curves to Summer. To smell it and find
your way back to the morning. To find your way
back to the light on the bed.

The cactus keeping its cool water secret
with a stillness you had once, long ago,
in a place where you laid down, but had to get up from,
to go on into your armourless life.

On Basketball

When the peach basket became too heavy
with potential, when the familiar in it
cracked and split like a panacea,
something broke free, buckled under the weight of what need had
    fastened,
and those who thought it didn't mean much to sink a jumper
learned how a good bounce could break the wood in them.

It took them years to cut a hole in the basket.
Maybe retrieval was the silent mantra
that peeled back the days of boredom like a callous.
Until the storm of limbs and taunts that sweated
upcourt was claimed by a new geography—
until disorder turned to questions turned to:
if any side delays the game, the umpire shall call foul;
the thrower-in is allowed five seconds;
allowance to be made for a player running at good speed.

On Betting Too Much Money in a Friendly Game of Cards

To go all in with little thinking, yes, their swagger,
yes, their confidence is a paper bridge and mine is the pickup truck
that will cross it.

    Even a seasoned player with a pair of kings
will lean back in the wiry chair of his uncertainty
and look over the stains on the ceiling.

Knowing that friendship like electricity
can be turned off, and knowing that the whole eastern seaboard
of your memory can be
    criss-crossed, shut down
        and started back up under new price structures—

    To hold a *coup d'état*
on what's precious—and later when the winnings have changed
hands so many times maybe they can't be won anymore—
wanting to crush them,
like the morning paper, like a handful of suds,
like a model town.

On Climbing a Ladder

Not climb but descend. Not descend but walk.
      Like standing with you at a Darwin exhibit,
sharing vodka by the plastic iguanas,
saying "I would name him Mike and him Charlie"—
      and not running out of money for the streetcar
home, hailing cabs of pessimism as night
comes on like a flat tire, and not the pigeons who aim their shit
like we have it coming. It's Spring
and I've lost so many umbrellas I don't know what to do with
    myself
but saunter down College, not strut, but wade, into the one-day sales
and the muggings and the kiosks and be here with you
                not fixed but
not willing exactly but by surprise.
Not the reams and reams of duct tape I would
need to keep our mail safe. Not to arrive.
We know that under every problem there is
    another problem and under that there is a kind of sea.
Spin and current. Every favourite song is a rung.

On Appreciating Space Exploration

Press your hands against the ceiling.
Notice how hot they become there on the border
of home and a sky that rolls like water
pushing its way through a hairline crack.

Step down slowly. Break a window.
Or, unravel a roll of film
then try to stuff it all back in the roll. Develop.

Spend a moment pondering this statement:
that the road should be built in this direction
or that direction is an equally preposterous notion.

Marry young. Acquire an appreciation of orbit
by making the same mistake over again
until it feels new, like an old shirt whose sleeves you roll up.

Try to wear that shirt around your legs. Try to fit
your arms around a full-grown oak.

Throw a fistful of marbles across a field.

Try to get inside a shoebox.

Fall off something.

On the Nuisance of Fires Started by Hand

Never big enough to warrant strict attention.
Started by boredom, accident, or fiat,
they either struggle and call it quits
or some unlikely turn of events
puts its lips to them and blows
and they grow tall, sinewy, they smoke:
an audience waiting for their band.

One might write the history
of fire very briefly: two things rubbing
in just the right way opened the lock
that let the sparks fly—and they went
on dropping propaganda.
Now you stand on the diving board
above your decision, above reply,

stiff shorts and fogged goggles
clinging tight. Here, depth perception
is done in by likeness; the deep end
seems as though you could breathe it.
That conspicuous lack of bleachers, space,
the flex of the fibreglass beneath
waving its sign of encouragement.

Simple Magnetic Overunity Toy

You can always blame friction. No matter how great your perpetual motion machine is, it will always produce friction and expel energy.
—Bob S., Yahoo! Answers

Ours was great! And only cost
ten dollars and twenty minutes to make.
And simple, too. No tins hanging from a rope
or mini-Ferris-wheel-of-weights
with different leverage.

The smallness of it was sublime:
a strip of magnets fanning out
and half a palm's worth of screws
we'd quarter-stripped in other designs
that hung now, flaccid, on their hooks.

If it worked, and somehow we'd jimmied
the lock on Newtonian drag,
the rest would puff out—that we knew.
Our old lives would jettison
from us like thrusters.

Though as the silver ball rolled upwards,
seeming to gather our skewed reflections
in lines that broke and fused back,
there was no snap,
no fall into some new recognition.

I thought of her, sealing
perishables for the cold,
her fingers squeezing the air
from where the air wanted to be.
The freezer that burned what it couldn't hold.

That way they'll last longer.
The ball had begun its loop again,

had slipped through the first chain of command
and was gathering force.
Tell me what we need to keep.

The Thought Box
after Ted Hughes

This moment's room is lit with track
lighting. There's no furniture.
Only a desk, this screen

where I type my words. A corner pokes
into view. Something is taking shape,
nailed together with hinges

that do not creak or rust.
Panels become more than panels,
placed together, now an enclosure.

The base leaves a print in the dust.
You can make shapes on the floor
no one has considered.

You can pick up the box and peer
inside, carry in it whatever you choose.
A lid shuts like a ban on lids.

In the mind, a box weighs
as much as an ocean, and both get bigger,
or smaller, or both.

Notes on the Poems

The epigraph for the first section is from *Song of Roland* (ed. Glyn Burgess, Penguin, 1990).

In "How the Tiktaalik Came onto Land," a tiktaalik is a prehistoric fish said to be the earliest evolutionary link between aquatic animals and land animals.

"Incongruous places often inspire anomalous stories" is the first sentence of the essay "Non-Overlapping Magisteria" by Stephen Jay Gould (*Skeptical Inquirer*, July 1999).

The epigram for the poem "Windows" is from Howard Nemerov's poem "Storm Windows" (ed. Donald Hall, *Contemporary American Poetry*, Penguin, 1962).

"I'll Climb the Tree If You Climb the Tree" was, in an early form, a centeo. The only still recognizable line is "I'll give a dollar even if the charge is fifty cents," which was adapted from a line in a David McFadden poem that I can no longer find. All other lines are original work and, thus, are not as good. No refunds.

The italicized lines in "On Basketball" are from the first draft of the rules of basketball by James Naismith. (From inventors. about.com)

Acknowledgements

Poems exact and in earlier versions appeared in *The Antigonish Review*, *Grain*, *This Magazine*, *Prairie Fire*, *The New Quarterly*, *The Malahat Review* and *The Walrus*. My thanks to the editors of these publications.

"Cactus Love" received the P. K. Page Founders' Award for 2007. "Eight Kinds of Knots" placed first in *This Magazine*'s Great Canadian Literary Hunt 2008. A selection from this collection was nominated for the Bronwen Wallace Award for 2008.

I'd like to acknowledge the support of the Ontario Arts Council in completing this book, through the Writers' Reserve program.

Additional special thanks to people who gave a read to some or all of these poems, recommended books or had another beer when it was time to go home. Brock, Cameron, De Mariaffi, Faulkner, Heroux, Mooney, Nash and Thran. Thanks to Ken Babstock and Dionne Brand for help with earlier drafts of this book. To my friend, editor and mentor Paul Vermeersch, who made these poems stronger and less frantic.